CAMBRIDGE LIBRARY COLLECTION

Books of enduring scholarly value

Archaeology

The discovery of material remains from the recent or the ancient past has always been a source of fascination, but the development of archaeology as an academic discipline which interpreted such finds is relatively recent. It was the work of Winckelmann at Pompeii in the 1760s which first revealed the potential of systematic excavation to scholars and the wider public. Pioneering figures of the nineteenth century such as Schliemann, Layard and Petrie transformed archaeology from a search for ancient artifacts, by means as crude as using gunpowder to break into a tomb, to a science which drew from a wide range of disciplines - ancient languages and literature, geology, chemistry, social history - to increase our understanding of human life and society in the remote past.

Archaeological Excavation

J. P Droop (1882–1963) was a classical field archaeologist. After graduating from Trinity College, Cambridge, in 1904 he worked as a field archaeologist for the British School at Athens, and was appointed Chair of Classical Archaeology at Liverpool University in 1914. This volume was intended as a guide to practical archaeological excavation and was first published in 1915 as part of the Cambridge Archaeological and Ethnological series. At the time of publication, archaeology was starting to become a more scientific and academic discipline, as can be seen in Droop's arguments on the importance of archaeological context and knowledge of stratification on site. The development of excavation as a scientifically based practice is shown by the emphasis on planning of the site, in contrast to earlier guides to excavation. This volume provides insights into the development of the theory as well as the practice of archaeology.

Cambridge University Press has long been a pioneer in the reissuing of out-of-print titles from its own backlist, producing digital reprints of books that are still sought after by scholars and students but could not be reprinted economically using traditional technology. The Cambridge Library Collection extends this activity to a wider range of books which are still of importance to researchers and professionals, either for the source material they contain, or as landmarks in the history of their academic discipline.

Drawing from the world-renowned collections in the Cambridge University Library, and guided by the advice of experts in each subject area, Cambridge University Press is using state-of-the-art scanning machines in its own Printing House to capture the content of each book selected for inclusion. The files are processed to give a consistently clear, crisp image, and the books finished to the high quality standard for which the Press is recognised around the world. The latest print-on-demand technology ensures that the books will remain available indefinitely, and that orders for single or multiple copies can quickly be supplied.

The Cambridge Library Collection will bring back to life books of enduring scholarly value (including out-of-copyright works originally issued by other publishers) across a wide range of disciplines in the humanities and social sciences and in science and technology.

Archaeological Excavation

J. P. DROOP

CAMBRIDGE
UNIVERSITY PRESS

CAMBRIDGE UNIVERSITY PRESS

Cambridge, New York, Melbourne, Madrid, Cape Town, Singapore,
São Paolo, Delhi, Dubai, Tokyo

Published in the United States of America by Cambridge University Press, New York

www.cambridge.org
Information on this title: www.cambridge.org/9781108010283

© in this compilation Cambridge University Press 2010

This edition first published 1915
This digitally printed version 2010

ISBN 978-1-108-01028-3 Paperback

This book reproduces the text of the original edition. The content and language reflect
the beliefs, practices and terminology of their time, and have not been updated.

Cambridge University Press wishes to make clear that the book, unless originally published
by Cambridge, is not being republished by, in association or collaboration with, or
with the endorsement or approval of, the original publisher or its successors in title.

Cambridge Archaeological and Ethnological Series

ARCHAEOLOGICAL
EXCAVATION

ARCHAEOLOGICAL EXCAVATION

BY

J. P. DROOP, M.A.
Late Student of the British School at Athens

Cambridge:

at the University Press

1915

CAMBRIDGE UNIVERSITY PRESS

C. F. CLAY, Manager

London: FETTER LANE, E.C.

Edinburgh: 100 PRINCES STREET

New York: G. P. PUTNAM'S SONS

Bombay, Calcutta and Madras: MACMILLAN AND Co., Ltd.

Toronto: J. M. DENT AND SONS, Ltd.

Tokyo: THE MARUZEN-KABUSHIKI-KAISHA

To

R. M. DAWKINS

" all-sagacious in our art,
Breeder in me of what poor skill I boast."

INTRODUCTION

THE time has perhaps gone by when it was necessary, if it ever were, to put forward a defence of the pleasant practice of digging, a defence of it, that is to say, not as a harmless recreation of the idle rich, but as a serious business for a reasonable man. In all ages the maker of history and the recorder of history have alike received due honour. To-day a place is found, not equal, of course, in glory but in the same hierarchy, for the reverent discoverer of the dry bones of history; and on Clio's roll of honour next to Homer and Agamemnon there is now a place for Schliemann.

In the last forty years excavation has been carried on very extensively in Italy, in Greece, and in Egypt, to say nothing of the work that has been done in the more northern countries of Europe, or in fields further to the east; and the time has come when it may be of some interest to set forth the principles that have been, or at least should have been, the basis of the work.

The reservation must be made; for in Greece, at least, and in Egypt it was unavoidably, but none the less deplorably, the case that the great men of the past lacked the experience that is now ours. Excavation, like surgery, is an art, but, unlike the surgeon, the excavator has no unlimited supply of new subjects ready to benefit by his growing skill. The number of sites that have been spoiled will not bear thinking of, sites that bring a vicarious remorse to the mind that remembers by what ignorance they were very lovingly but very shamefully mishandled, so that their secrets, instead of being gathered up, were spilled and lost. The pity of it is that in the old days excavation was not recognised as an art; the excavator took a spade and dug and what he found he found; what could be more simple or more satisfying? To-day he knows, or should know, for the reservation is again necessary, that what he finds is not more important than the conditions in which he finds it. On the old plan it is as if a man were shown the symbols $(a + b)$ $(a - b)$ and, when asked what he saw, replied: $a + b$ and $a - b$. There is no intention here of suggesting that all the great men of the past were fools and that wisdom has been reserved for the present generation; far from it, but in a business in which accumulated experience joined with common sense carries a man three-quarters of the way the results in the days of no experience were of necessity much as if it had been so.

The writer's training has been entirely gained in Greek lands, with the addition of one season in Egypt, so that any illustrations with which he may point his remarks must be drawn from a comparatively narrow field, but he believes that the broad principles that should underlie archaeological excavation do not vary with locality, and this all the more because one of them is that the nature of every site must be taken into careful consideration before any lessons can be safely drawn from the yield of the work.

From the stress laid in the following pages upon stratification the reader might be excused for thinking that all sites have been stratified by past generations with a nice comprehension of the needs of the excavator. Unfortunately it is not so. Many sites show no strata and in many more the strata that once existed have been destroyed by rash digging for foundations or by other baleful activities, though ancient builders were not so criminal as their modern successors. But because where strata do not exist digging is easy, and because where strata do exist digging is most difficult and the results of digging most fruitful in knowledge, I believe that to be able to dig a stratified site well is to have attained to the highest and most remunerative skill in this particular work; therefore I make no apology for laying stress on the importance of stratification; its presence should always be assumed until the worst is known, for no scientific harm is done by the assumption and much may be saved. It need hardly be said that this refers only to the process of digging, not to the subsequent study of the finds; for the man who worked out his results on the assumption that his finds must have been stratified would soon make a great, but not an enviable, name. The fact is, of course, easy to ascertain as the excavation proceeds, chiefly by the consistency or otherwise of the results; consistency is the main point, and too much faith should never be given to isolated phenomena, even if not contradicted, for nothing is more necessary to remember than that any individual object or set of objects may have got out of place. One or two iron knife-blades were found mixed with the Middle Minoan pottery at the cave above Kamares, yet we forbore to proclaim to the world that the Middle Minoans were an iron-using people; there, however, there was no stratification to be contaminated, but sometimes the most scandalous finds turn up; a mediaeval coin, for instance, has been known to try to compromise the purest of neolithic deposits.

This essay has been written with the idea chiefly of entertaining the many who by their interest and subscriptions have helped in the work of recovering the past, and partly in the hope that, if it makes even slightly for the accomplishment of better work in the future, it may not have been written in vain; and the writer has dared to put his views with the more freedom because he has never been in charge of an excavation, and therefore need not fear the reproach that what he preaches he did not practise.

Lastly—at the present time such a book as this should not appear without an apology for its impertinence; yet this will perhaps seem less gross to those who look confidently to a future in which we shall be free once more to care about the past.

J. P. D.

London.
August 1915.

CONTENTS

FIGURES

CHAPTER I

GENERAL

The archaeologist's general aim on approaching a new site should be to draw from it all the knowledge that he can, to unearth as complete a skeleton as possible of the history of that particular spot during the period when it was a human habitation. Unless that period belongs to times when men wrote what can now be read, he can hardly hope to uncover perfect history, but the more complete the dry bones that he lays bare the better the chance that they will rise again as history when imagination shall have prophesied to them.

Therefore the excavator's sympathies should be as wide as possible, and nothing that he finds should meet with his neglect because it is not just what he is looking for. This sounds obvious and most unnecessary to be said, yet, to take but one instance of a breach of this rule, there are to-day archaeologists with well-known names who will dig a site only for its inscriptions, paying no attention to other and in their eyes lesser finds. This is a double crime, a crime against the actual neglected finds and a crime against the site and its possible treasures yet unfound. It should always be remembered that in general a site cannot be touched and left without irreparable damage, and that there can hardly be a worse sin for an excavator than having attacked a site to leave the part begun unfinished. Yet this is likely to be the result of an interest that is insufficiently catholic.

It is a lesser evil, but I think generally a mistake, even to leave a separate part of a site for operations in the indefinite future, unless the circumstances are very favourable and there is definite reason to think the course beneficial. There are I think two reasons against it. In the first place, there is the great importance of establishing the relative positions of the things found and the fact that it is never very easy to settle accurately the relations between old and new. And secondly to begin a site and to leave it diminishes the potential interest of the part undug, and lessens the chances of the work's ever being finished unless a particular set of circumstances should again direct attention to the place. It is however only fair to mention one instance (Phylakopi in the island of Melos excavated 1896–1898 and again 1911) where this practice was in the result very beneficial. The circumstances were however particularly favourable, for it was a town site and the undug portion was neatly partitioned off by the walls of the houses. The advantages of the supplementary dig were due to the knowledge of Cretan pottery gained in the interval, which knowledge made the study of the finds easier. All the same had the first excavation been the ideal piece of work that we never hope to see there would have been no need of a second.

I am not, of course, arguing that an unproductive site should be dug to the bitter end.

That were to ask too much of human nature. Moreover in such a case the presumption would be that there is nothing there to be damaged by abandonment.

To resume, in theory nothing that is found is without interest and everything should be dealt with. For many facts that appear to have no interest at the time may become of first-rate importance in the future through the discovery of similar facts elsewhere. The same excavation of Phylakopi gives an example in the case of the so-called "Minyan" ware. At the time of the first excavation this ware was practically unknown and received a bare mention in the publication, though the results of the second excavation suggest that it must have been found in considerable quantities. This was no doubt due to its apparent inferiority of interest where so much was new and of first-rate importance. By a piece of good fortune the second excavation in 1911 was able to supplement the first, and to find out several points vital to the history of this ware, which but for this chance might have been lost entirely owing to the former omission to put them on record. I do not wish to say anything in disparagement of the treatment of the pottery at the earlier excavation, still less to appear to patronise it, but my comment on it will lead up to the next point that I wish to make. It was a very good piece of work indeed but it was not ideal (if it had been there would have been little need of the second excavation, notwithstanding the new knowledge of Cretan pottery acquired in the interval), and the chief reason why it was not ideal was that there was too much material for one man to deal with really adequately. My impression of the whole of that first excavation, on which three seasons were spent, is that the excavators cleared too much of the town in the time, they went too fast and were swamped by their material.

The staff should be adequate and the work should not proceed too fast. Naturally these two factors, the speed of the work and the numbers of the staff, are interdependent. No excavation can be really well done if it is not possible to keep abreast of the finds, that is to say, to ascertain pretty well what is being found as the work proceeds.

It is to be hoped that the days are over when extensive digs were carried on by one or two men, the days when it was possible without shame and only partly in jest to say that one of the charms of winter work in the museum was the rediscovery of what had been found at the excavation—the days, in fine, when a spirit of madness was abroad that actually led men to adopt and act on the following creed: "Wherever it is feasible, the employment of large gangs of men is more economical and more conducive to accurate archaeological observation, than the employment of smaller numbers of men spread over a longer period of time. The manner, for instance, in which the various archaeological stratifications......present themselves in rapid and organic succession to the eye of the student, when work is carried on on a large scale, adds a quality to the mode of observation which cannot readily be supplied when work is less compressed in time." The last sentence is perfectly true but the name of that quality is confusion.

I hope and believe that those days are over; yet many excavations must depend unfortunately too much on the support of public subscriptions, so that the temptation is strong to widen the scope of the work in order that the increased results may keep alive the interest of subscribers; on a productive site the tendency should be checked, because it will always lead to a passing of the limits beyond which the work loses in efficiency, will always lead in fact to the process known by the expressive name of "hogging." The need of an adequate staff applies equally to the subsequent study of the finds in the museum. Every effort should be made to get such study and the publication of its results done as quickly as possible without loss of thoroughness. In the case of work depending for its support on public interest this is obvious common sense, but apart from that, loss of time means definite loss shown in the results, definite loss of knowledge. For in this imperfect world with the passage of time comes the mislaying and shifting of labels, and the most perfect notes become less intelligible when the memory of the context that should illumine them has faded. The initiated could point to several great excavations which are believed to have suffered much through being dealt with subsequently by too small a staff. All this, like most things connected with my subject, is common sense. Any work to be done efficiently needs an adequate staff. The too frequent neglect of this point in past archaeology either points to personal selfishness in high places or merely goes to show that it was not yet recognised that there are two ways of conducting an excavation. Finally it is clear that the best way of ensuring enough helpers in the museum is to have enough on the dig; not only will their interest be engaged so that they will be eager to assist in the work of publication, but other things being equal that work will be better done by the men who saw all the conditions of the finding.

The last general principle to be mentioned has again no peculiar application to archaeology. It is the need for good organisation, necessary in arranging the actual work of digging and still more necessary in dealing with the finds.

For the excavator of a productive site is much in the position of a general in the field who is receiving a constant stream of fresh troops. In both cases the arrivals are very welcome, but without proper organisation the result is disastrous confusion.

Thus the man who means to undertake a dig should know the necessity of having an interest as catholic as possible, and besides a sense of duty to his finds, whether they happen to stir his interest or not, of realising the calls that the site will make on his resources, and of holding his hand if he feels that they will be such as in the future he may not be able to honour, of securing enough helpers both during and after the excavation, and lastly of never allowing his natural human eagerness to tempt him to go so fast as to risk the breakdown of his organisation.

CHAPTER II

A. *Digging.*

General principles it is easy enough to state, but the matter is not so simple when it comes to the particular question, By what means are objects best found and made to yield up their story? The answer comes in the form of another principle nearly as general as its predecessors. An excavation should be so conducted that it would be possible in theory to build up the site again with every object replaced exactly in its original position. For it is not until after excavation has disclosed fully what may be called the geological nature of the site, the original contours of the virgin soil, and the source and order of the subsequent accumulations, that reasoned conclusions can be formed as to the history of the objects found; and these conclusions cannot be formed, or at least cannot be formed with the same certainty, if the relations of the individual finds either with one another or with the geological conditions are not accurately known. Should the objects have been taken out in a higgledy-piggledy manner no subsequent knowledge of the history of the accumulations will be of much avail, and instead of having evidence from stratification the student will be reduced to evidence from style. And this may mean that all that he can say with certainty about the site will be the fruit of his previous knowledge. I say that the student will be reduced to the evidence from style, using the verb deliberately as implying a natural inferiority inherent in that kind of evidence. As an excavator I wish to insist on this point because we are engaged in upsetting the old gods, and we still have to fight for our new creed; for as yet there have not been enough good stratified sites properly dug to carry its truth into universal acceptance. Men are conservative in their religions, and the habit of offering incense on the altar of style is of very old origin; since collectors existed long before the scientific excavator, and have long been forming conclusions about their possessions by the only means open to them; consequently the new truth has a formidable antagonist in the old habit of mind, particularly with those to whom the facts of an excavation are unfamiliar. It behoves me therefore to set it down as plainly as I can that, when the evidence from excavation, the evidence, that is, for the chronology of a set of objects founded on a mass of observations as to how they lay, comes as may happen into conflict with the views on the subject derived from a study of the style of those objects, by tracing their probable development from one stage to another with the support of wide-drawn analogies—when these two radically different kinds of evidence come into conflict the opposed forces are not equal; it is not permitted us to say that the two discrepant witnesses exactly balance one another, so that we must reserve an open mind. The truth is that the two kinds of evidence are so far from balancing that the stylistic conclusions formed perhaps on *a priori* grounds and to a large extent subjective must be outweighed by those attested by the hard facts of observed stratification; for men may be mistaken in their views on the development of form and ornament, but to discredit in favour of these the evidence of a good piece of stratification observed by competent persons is to abandon the scientific attitude and to proclaim a real faith vigorous and impregnable before the assaults of reason.

I would not however be understood to give less than their value to the conclusions to be drawn from a wide study of style when better evidence is not to be had: I believe indeed that such a conflict as I have indicated would be rare, and that in most cases where excavation has been able to form a check the conclusions from both sources have been found to tally. Yet one such conflict can be found (if I may be allowed the egotism of calling attention to a piece of work in which I had a share), in two papers dealing with the "Cyrenaic" vases that are scattered through the museums of Europe[1]. Both these papers attempted a chronological classification of the vases in question, and they will be found by the curious to differ widely. M. Dugas' paper was much the more skilful piece

---

[1] Dugas, *Rev. Arch.* 1907, Tom. IX, p. 403; Droop, *J. H. S.* xxx, p. 1.

of work, for he had nothing to go on but the
sharpness of his eyesight and a wide knowledge of
the development of vase-painting elsewhere; my
classification, on the other hand, needed only an
intimate acquaintance with one set of vases,
namely the large and very well stratified mass of
fragments of the same ceramic fabric that we were
lucky enough to find at Sparta just after M. Dugas
had written his paper; the whole history of the
ware was there before me divided into its stages
by the stratification, and all that I had to do with
the vases known before was to slip each into its
proper division. The reason for the breakdown of
the argument from style in this case is not uninter-
esting. It was not then known that these vases
were made in Laconia (the fact is not even yet
universally admitted, but they were); consequently no one had thought of seeing in them the
peculiar effects of the Spartan ideals. Yet we now
know that in the eighth and early seventh centuries
art showed as fair a blossom at Sparta as anywhere
else in Greece, but began to wither there at the
close of the seventh century under the blight of
militarism. On the pottery the effect was that
the style of drawing never passed the archaic
stage; throughout the sixth century the work got
progressively worse and more careless, and lacked
the impulse to develop greater freedom so that it
ended as archaic as it began; small wonder then
that the most careful student of style being without
the key should be deceived into placing very
careless and archaic-looking work much earlier
than is warranted by its fabric, which we now

know to be almost the only guide to the dating
of the Laconian vases. It is due to M. Dugas to
say that his prompt acceptance of the Sparta
results shows him not to be a man to whom
evidence from excavation makes a weak appeal.

   Revenons à nos moutons. The only way by
which an approximation to this desired accurate
knowledge of the relative positions of finds can be
reached is by subdivision of the site, minute subdivision both vertically and horizontally. The
limits of the horizontal subdivisions are often fore-
ordained by walls, but, if these do not exist or are
not close enough together, arbitrary divisions must
be made. Vertical divisions are also sometimes
provided ready to hand, as for instance the floors
of a house. But these, even should they exist,
are not always easily detected in the actual digging
unless they consist of stone slabs or cobbles. It
is true that afterwards traces of them can fre-
quently be detected in section in the walls, but
then unless other steps have been taken it might
be difficult to decide, however beautifully the order
of the successive finds was preserved, at what point
in that order the floor level came. There is one
well-known excavation where such a point always
remained in doubt.

   The only way in which the vertical relations of
the objects found can be properly ascertained is
by using a dumpy level continually all over the
site[1]. The method is simple though laborious.
The horizontal sections being marked out, the men
are set to dig, and are shown a depth to which

----

[1] See Appendix A.

they should dig evenly over the extent of their
section. The levels of the top and the bottom of
the section are taken and are written, together
with the horizontal designation, on the labels
attached to all finds from that section. Suppose
then that digging had gone on in room 1 of house A
in a prehistoric town, and that subsequently
remains of a clay flooring were observed in the
sides of the pit, a change of soil being there
discernible, although during the actual digging it
had passed unnoticed. The level of it is taken
and found to be 90·35 m. A reference to the finds
shows one set of objects from A1 90·50—90·30 and
the next below from A1 90·31—90·09. This no
doubt is not so satisfactory as if the floor had been
detected at once and made the bottom of a division
or had by chance coincided with one, but it is a
good deal better than nothing.

Of course, it is not on every site that vertical
divisions so small as ·20 m. repay the trouble:
often ·50 m. or even more will answer every
purpose; but, until trial has been made, work
should always be begun on the supposition that
minute subdivision will be necessary to catch all
changes in the deposits. The thickness of section
allowable is in direct ratio to the rate at which
the "pay dirt" was deposited; it is clear for
example that on the site of a rich shrine the
deposits of votive offerings would be laid down
faster and over a given length of years would
reach a greater thickness than at one comparatively poor; wherefore, the development of style
and fashion in the offerings being assumed to be

uniform, at a poor site the changes due to such
development would be found closer together, in
other words the strata would be more compressed,
so that to make sure of catching the different
stages of development the vertical sections must
then be made thinner. Suppose that at a rich
site the deposits of style A and B each attained
the thickness of ·50 m., sections of that thickness
might be counted on to record them, but at a
poor site the same deposits might only reach a
thickness of ·25 m. each, in which case sections of
·50 m. would be in danger of showing A and B as
contemporaneous; there might be suspicion of the
true state of the case but there would be no
certainty. The slower, then, the rate of deposit
the thinner must be the sections.

It should be remarked here that the use of the
level does not imply a hasty generalisation that
what is higher up must needs be later in date than
what is below. This may, perhaps, be found true
of any particular pit, but it is not to be pre-
supposed even there, and far less over the whole
site. It is merely a device for preserving the data
so that after the end of the excavation all the
evidence from which to draw the proper conclusions
may be at hand. With such an ideal it is clearly
important to dig methodically, taking off layer by
layer so far as possible over the whole of that part
of the site that is being dealt with at one time,
though nothing is more difficult than to prevent
an untrained workman from digging a hole instead
of taking an even layer off the whole of his section.
This point is clearly of the first importance for

establishing the position of finds properly, for if it is neglected there is a danger that the levels taken may not tell a true story of the section as a whole. From this point of view, indeed, keeping the whole of one part of the site more or less on the same level is not of very great importance, but the avoidance of deep digging here and there in general simplifies the arrangement of roads for dumping and makes it always easier to work from the top.

The necessity for so working in order to gain our methodical end is obvious, but it needs emphasizing, for there is always a great temptation for the workman to dig from the side inwards—it is easier and saves him a great deal of labour. Instead of lifting every spadeful all that he has to do is a little undermining, and the upper earth comes down of itself. It is however the gravest of crimes, for it insures the confusion of any stratification that may have existed. It might be argued that if all that is necessary to salvation is so to dig by subdivisions that in theory everything could be put back in position, this result could be got just as well by having a big vertical and a very small horizontal section. It is not so however, for such an argument would ignore the original workings of time whereby in nine cases out of ten the knowledge that is valuable concerns the vertical position of objects, not the horizontal. Moreover, whereas digging from the top permits of full control at will of the dimensions of sections both horizontal and vertical, digging from the side leaves little control of the vertical dimensions of the section, which would practically depend on the height of the earth wall that is being attacked.

Fatal to the knowledge of stratification, digging from the side is not to be recommended even when it is certain that there is none to know, for unless the excavation is taking place on a hillside the practice involves more labour, not to the actual man with the spade, but to the excavation as a whole. For should a track on the level be necessary for the removal of the dump, to allow any soil to fall further than can be helped is clear waste of labour. During my season in Egypt the application of labour to the bottom of a mound that had to be cleared must have wasted a large amount of work, for by that method it is hardly an exaggeration to say that all the sand first slid down to the very lowest point possible, the bottom of the mound, which was lower than the surrounding desert, and thence had to be carried up to the dumping railway on the level of the desert. If the work had been applied to the top of the mound much money might have been saved. There however the only harm was wasted money, on a stratified site the penalty would have been lost possibilities of knowledge.

If time and money were of no account there is no doubt that for a productive site the best digging tool would be a kind of bread-knife without a point. The use of such a weapon goes nearest to insure the fewest possible breakages, for it is light, and the blunt end does not provide the same strong temptation as a point to use premature leverage. Excavators however are only human so that it is in practice impossible to forbear the use of pick and spade until it is known that objects lie so thick that the knife must be substituted. And then I think the governing reason is the fear rather of missing than of breaking objects. The question of breakages is very delicate. There is naturally a strong desire to keep them down and to eliminate all unnecessary smashes, but in practice it is not found advisable to punish such or even to give severe reprimands, for such unpleasantness gives the workman strong reason to suppress in future all traces of his victim—a far worse evil.

Rather to be recommended is an appeal to the man's better nature, supported by what is perhaps still more effective, a reduction but not complete suppression of the tip, when the object is such as would naturally produce one. Where more firmness can be shown with advantage is when a piece is missing from an object and the break shows new, a matter about which there can seldom be doubt. Rigorous search can well be insisted on, for, though no doubt the man regards it as a nuisance, nothing irremediable has happened, so that the only temptation towards complete suppression is laziness, which the certain loss of the possible tip may be trusted to check.

The system of tips here referred to, which has worked well in Greece, consists of giving a ticket to the finder of any object thought worth it. The giver writes on it the nature of the object and initials it, and on pay-day it is redeemed for such a sum, varying in practice from twenty centimes to a franc, as he thinks it worth. The men seem to like the system, the element of chance in the uncertain value of the ticket being a great attraction, and it has this great merit that it wonderfully sharpens the workman's eyes.

Sharpness of the eyes, which is really responsive quickness of the brain, is perhaps for the excavator the greatest of nature's gifts, though it can be improved by practice. Where it is probably most needed is for the noting of all changes of soil as the digging proceeds. These may mean nothing, but they may mean everything, as in the case of the layer of sand at the Sanctuary of Orthia at Sparta. They are, unless well marked and general, the most elusive of observable facts, and once missed they may offer no second chance of detection, but a comparison of a series of such observations over a whole site may tell a great story. I see no reason against keeping a specimen of the soil of every section except the extra trouble, nine-tenths of which would, of course, be wasted, but which would be well repaid later on by the possibility of checking the field observations. One point that should never be forgotten is the usefulness of making diagrams of the stratification and changes in the earth when such are visible in the sides of trenches and pits. For instance, supposing that it were possible to make the subjoined drawings, Figs. 1 and 2, showing the changes in the earth and finds observed in the sides of two trenches at right angles to one another along the lines $B—A$, $C—B$, as in Fig. 3, it would be possible to deduce from these with some certainty the rough contours of the virgin soil in this neighbourhood (indicated in Fig. 3 by the figures in metres), and, from noticing how the deposits so far from following that contour line rise steeply towards the point B, to guess that something of exceptional interest should lie in that direction to account for this swelling. The hint so obtained would be of material value when the whole area came to be cleared, and the observations would in any case be useful later on as a check to the levels taken,

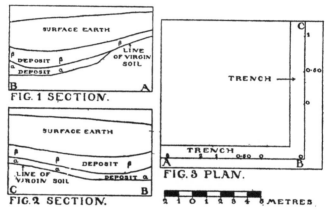

FIG. 1 SECTION.

FIG. 2 SECTION.

FIG. 3 PLAN.

Specimen sketches of Stratification.

and as a help to the understanding of the history of the deposits. It was by working on these lines that the excavators at Sparta were able to guess beforehand at the existence of the early temple at the Sanctuary of Orthia and to be, so to speak, ready for it[1]. And, however much care theory demands for all stages of the operations, in practice a special whip of this kind has its usefulness. The workmen should of course be trained to report at

[1] *B. S. A.* XIV, pp. 13 and 14.

once any change in the soil that they may notice,
as they would any thrilling find, but as workmen
are not to be trusted to pay attention to such
trifles, which being beyond their understanding
they treat as mere whims of their employer, the
employer's eye should never be far off.   It follows
then that no excavation should ever be left without
some capable man in charge, and work should
never be carried on over an area wider than can
be supervised properly.   For given the chance any
site will develop enough spiteful intelligence to
produce its best finds just in the absence of the
observing eye, and even among the best trained
workmen there are few with self-restraint enough
to wait for its return.   When authority does return
it may be to find an urn burial with the vase
already moved, and the chance of photographing
or sketching it in position gone.

This is a return to the plea for an adequate
staff.   It is also a plea for comparatively short
hours.   As thus: in Greece when a man is engaged
to work he expects to do so from 6 a.m. to 6 p.m.,
with half an hour for breakfast at 8, and an hour
and a half off in the middle of the day, or if it is
getting towards summer he will work till 6.30 with
two hours' rest at noon.   Those hours he would
work tilling his own fields or another's, and exca-
vating work is on the whole less heavy, for pick
and spade naturally rest by turns, the spade being
never used for breaking up the soil but only for
clearing away that already excavated.   The man in
charge however has his attention continually on the
strain.   Moreover his headquarters are generally

not absolutely on the site, and even at lunch time the journey to and fro may leave him little time for rest if he is to be back when work begins, while at breakfast time this is manifestly impossible. And, however adequately staffed the excavation may be, to have another man ready to go out when the first returns does not pay, apart from the unsociability and the possible culinary difficulties, because in work of this kind if anything is happening the reliever should always overlap the relieved in order that he may be brought up to date with the position. I am convinced that a lengthening of the morning and midday rests would greatly increase the efficiency of the man in charge, and would probably mean a decrease in slackness in the workman towards the end of the day, so that the actual loss in amount of work done would not be great. It is no doubt, in the case of excavations dependent on subscriptions, a desire to get the utmost possible in return for the money spent that is responsible for the length of the hours of work, but these are, nevertheless, a mistake, for they lead to staleness. It is open however to the reader to ascribe this view of mine to laziness.

B. *Trials.*

With wealth, unlimited time and superhuman patience a man might work out his subdivisions and proceed. Few, unfortunately, can afford to do so. For the rest it is necessary to make trials before beginning the main work, which is a pity because a site is not a cheese and tastes are apt to damage it.

If there are walls showing or stones that look like parts of walls it is a natural, and strange to say quite proper, method of beginning trials to dig trenches along them to discover how deep they go. If there are no walls, it is better to dig trenches than a series of pits in spite of the greater cost, for the absence of gaps in the line gives a certainty that no transverse wall has been missed. The danger of trusting to pits is illustrated by the story that some pits that were dug in the middle of the Palace of Knossos missed everything [1]. If then the presence of a building is suspected, and most sites possess buildings, two pairs of trenches at right angles to one another across the given area to be tried should have a good chance of finding it, and would at least limit absolutely the space still open for search in that area. In rocky countries where field divisions are often stone walls, it is well to remember that these may be built on ancient foundations.

All trenches should be dug with as much care and subdivision as the subsequent excavation as soon as finds have declared themselves, and their position should be carefully planned. No matter how unpromising the outlook every trial trench should be carried down to virgin soil, for the excavator cannot otherwise be sure that he has obtained all the knowledge possible from that trench. This indeed applies to main operations just as much as to trials, though perhaps the temptation is strongest to abandon a barren trench.

[1] *B.S.A.* viii, p. 1.

This again is a principle that has only to be stated to be admitted, but there is more than one famous Greek site where a resumption of work at a later period has revealed unsuspected spoils at a depth never reached in the earlier operations. Curiously enough the two cases that are in my mind at the moment were both in the hands of those apostles of thoroughness, the Germans.

A method of testing the ground exhaustively that has been put forward is to run a series of trenches alongside one another, filling each as it is finished with the earth dug from the new one. It is a very easy way for there is not much lifting of earth involved, and no carting except that of the earth from the first trench, which must in the end be moved across to fill the last. I hope this method has been buried long ago, but as there is always a risk of its being resurrected, I enter a warning. It has nothing to recommend it. It is a thoroughly messy way of digging (whoever has read so far will see that this alone is enough to condemn it), for instead of the minimum that should be aimed at it involves the maximum of standing earth wall, through digging in a series of narrow strips; a very bad thing, as it always means a chance that the stratification may become mixed through small objects falling or being washed out of the sides of the trench at the upper levels, and being confused with the finds from lower down. Moreover the open trench by the side of that being dug provides a tempting opportunity for the crime of digging in from the side. And the method is not even so cheap as it looks, for it probably requires more trenches than are necessary to find out that the site is not worth digging. Should the contrary appear no one I think would continue the method. I believe the most plausible defence is likely to be that it is a way combining cheapness and thoroughness of searching for some particular wall or building, the presence of which is suspected. If all that is wanted is to find the building, there is no more to be said, but if, as may be presumed, it is desired to excavate the building when found, I submit that it is not a good thing to set to work by a preliminary mess-up of its surroundings. There is however one occasion, and only one, when I would admit the method, and that is when a cemetery is being sought for, and there is no reason to suppose that the area contains anything else. For isolated trenches may easily miss tombs.

When trials have settled the area to be dug they are not finished with, for the best site for the dump has yet to be chosen and when chosen to be tested before work is begun. For economically it is sheer waste of money to throw soil on a place from which it may have to be moved, and archaeo-logically it is criminal, for the added cost will afterwards always act as a deterrent from digging such a spot.

C. *Dumping.*

About dumping there is not much that is useful to be said. The problem is always to adjust the means to the requirements. The means within my knowledge are an overhead railway on ropes, a light railway with trucks (man or horse drawn),

carts, wheel-barrows and baskets. The first two
perhaps hardly repay the trouble unless the amount
of soil to be moved is very great, or the only
proper site for the dump very distant; moreover,
unless the plant is large it is probably not feasible
to bring them right up to several scattered points
of work, and another method such as baskets must
be used to feed the railway from various points.
All this may be very satisfactory in certain circumstances as when a large amount of what is known
to be unproductive soil has to be moved to a
distance. If however the site is one productive
of small and easily overlooked objects, however
extensive it may be there are at least two reasons
for preferring a method of dumping, perhaps less
rapid, but more easily controlled. The first is
that, whereas the soil should be raked through
with the hand before removal, the larger the
receptacle the greater the tendency to fill it as
rapidly as possible without paying the soil that
attention. This may seem rather a fanciful point,
but I have always thought that one of the reasons
why the second season's work at a certain famous
excavation had to consist partly of the digging of
the first season's dump was the tempting ease
with which the earth could be tipped over the
hillside. However that may be it is very certain
that the greater the amount tipped over the dump
at one go the less easy it is to notice anything
that ought not to be there. However careful the
digger is it is always worth while to have a boy
looking over the newly tipped dump, and the
smaller the individual tippings the more hopeful

his task.   The next point is that the less elaborate
the dumping system the easier it is to modify, if
the quantity and minuteness of the finds make it
necessary to sieve all earth from certain sections
before dumping.   When this happens, of course,
the earth from each section and level must be
labelled accordingly, and sieved separately that
any finds from it may not lose their context.
Now, it is perfectly true that if it is decided to
be necessary the trouble entailed will be borne,
but it is none the less certain that the question
presents itself in the form, Is it worth while?
Thus the more complex the system to be altered
the greater the unconscious check on a step otherwise perhaps advisable.

I confess to a certain shrinking, perhaps irra-
tional, from the more wholesale methods of
dumping.   I would rather see my work held up
slightly while I arranged for increased facilities to
meet the proved demands of the site, than have
my means of dumping greater than necessary, for
there is, I think, in that case a danger not wholly
fanciful of a subtle change in the excavator's
point of view, of his coming to regard the dumping
cars as voracious monsters that must be fed, and
the amount of soil moved as the standard of his
achievements.

D.   *First Aid.*

It does not need much experience for a man to
tell when an object is too fragile to stand being
taken from the earth unsupported.   Indeed, I
think experience tells the other way and leads to

greater boldness. The necessary support may be given in two ways, either by plaster of Paris or by paraffin wax. As much soil is removed from the surface and all round the object as is possible without disturbing it. Then in the first process it is covered with wet paper and plaster not mixed too thin is poured over and round it. When the plaster has set, it is generally possible to cut the object loose from beneath without breaking it, as the support above prevents the usual upheaval. After removal, the lower surface of the object should be cleaned and also supported by plaster, after which the upper plaster can be removed and the upper surface cleaned. By this means the object is never unsupported during the process of cleaning. If the use of paraffin wax is preferred, all that is needed is a spirit lamp and a frying pan. The wax is melted and poured on in as many coats as seem required by the weight of the object. If it is not proposed to clean the object at once the back should also be coated after removal. To remove the wax remelting is all that is necessary. There is not much to choose between the two methods, for while it is easier to leave a support during the process of cleaning if plaster is used, there is less chance of breaking the object by melting the wax than by sawing the plaster to remove it. These devices are only practical with comparatively small objects, but luckily the fragile as a rule runs small.

The excavator however soon learns to be philosophical about breakages, whether old or new. If he did not he could not bear his trade. Some indeed bring their philosophy to such a pitch as to feel that the better view is to prefer things broken, that to put a premium on the unbroken object smacks rather of the collector, that all that the best people should care about is knowledge, and that they should be satisfied if enough is left to show the original nature of the whole. They do not however carry their theories so far into practice as to neglect any means of preserving what does happen to be perfect. It is little enough as a rule.

E. *Notes.*

To take notes at an excavation is in itself an art to be learnt. It is not easy to write a description that shall omit nothing of importance and be intelligible to another person or to the writer himself six months afterwards when the context has faded from his mind. In this connection there is a further advantage in the division of the site into sections, for it provides at once a heading for the note, and the writer is not left wondering how to fix the position of the fact he is to describe. It is impossible to give directions for such notes, but they should err in the direction of fullness rather than of concision, and it is well to remember that rough sketches and plans are often worth more than a good many words.

In practice the excavator's vocabulary is probably full of slang words and nicknames for particular classes of finds. There is, I think, no reason why he should put himself to the pains of translating the words that come to his mind, the

use of which may often mean a real saving of
space and time, provided that he chooses a leisure
moment to enter a dictionary on a spare page;
I possess for instance a notebook from Sparta
that records the presence in many sections of
"Toutou" in varying quantities. "Some have
greatness thrust upon them," among whom was
Geórgios Toutoudákis or Toutoús. He was a
Cretan who worked at Sparta during the first
season, and he it was who working in a pit by
himself found the first specimens of pottery of a
particular period, the relations of which at that
time could only be guessed at. What more natural
than to call it after its finder? The ware in
question has since become known as Laconian V,
but it was two and a half years before we had
sufficient evidence on which to classify the Spartan
pottery, during which years Toutou's name was
on our lips to an extent that would have surprised
him. It was short and distinctive, and answered
every purpose while the proper name of the said
ware yet remained hidden. If any finds are connected with the circumstances noted it is often
useful to add to their label a reference to the page
in the notebook. Lastly to provide for the worst
the handwriting and arrangement should be intelligible not to the writer only.

It has often been said, and not without a
certain truth, that the best notes are labels.
Circumstances no doubt vary with climates but
in Europe the plan that works best is to use a
label of wood and to write on it with not too
soft a pencil. In Greece the wooden label is

particularly useful as it checks the depredations of
an insect rife in all local museums whose favourite
delicacy is paper and particularly inky paper.
Unless the pencil used is too soft the wooden label
is also indifferent to a wetting, and it has the
advantage, or at least the compensation for its
initial expense, that after the complete study and
probable concentration of the finds, and the consequent discharge from their functions of many
labels, these can be made ready for new service
by the use of sandpaper. A string-hole should be
provided for the attachment of the label to isolated
finds or to the basket or tray. Workmen who are
finding objects should be trained to look on a
label duly written and issued by authority as their
most crying need, and to think that to be found
content without a label is a crime only surpassed
by confounding the belongings of two separate
labels.

I once saw an excavation where the finds of
pottery in different years were distinguished by
dabs of different coloured paint. The advantage
of making such a distinction was not very apparent
but the system appeared to have valuable possibilities when applied to stratification. Clearly
there are practical difficulties in the way of applying
it to minute subdivision, but as the work proceeds
should certain clear divisions in the stratification
be shown by well-defined landmarks, the system
might well be used to mark off the contents of
these divisions, not to supersede labels but as a
safeguard against their displacement; or again it
would be invaluable in the case of a building

yielding wall-fresco fragments in great quantity from its different parts; for the fitting together of such is a puzzle that may take years to accomplish, years in which accidents might befall the best system of labelling; in such a case much virtue would lie in a series of indelible marks that would always show in what part of the building were found the individuals of a crowd of similar pieces.

The keeping of an excavation day-book is sometimes thought advisable. In an extensive excavation where different regions are under separate direction it might be useful to secure that an account of the work as a whole should be found between one set of covers. In practice however it happens that reference is seldom made to the day-book, each man preferring to refer to his own notes, and what is felt to be the useless labour of writing it up every night becomes a great burden. The better plan would seem to keep such a book for entering once a week or once a fortnight not the details of every day, which are safe enough elsewhere, but the general trend of the excavation, and the broad conclusions drawn from the work accomplished to date, things which do not make their way into the field notebook. Indeed the only real advantage of the daily plan is that it leads the writer to think over the results of the day, and to clear up on the spot any ambiguity in his notes. But for this a day-book is not necessary.

F. *Site-choosing.*

"This is all very well" I can hear my reader saying, supposing that he has got so far, "but we know that the recipe for roast hare properly begins 'First catch your hare' and we have heard nothing about that yet." The truth of the matter is that there is not very much to say about the catching of the hare. I sometimes think, indeed, that people credit the excavator with dealings in black magic or at least with the use of a divining rod; for the question that I have met most often is "How do you know where to dig?" The answer is "By using our eyes and ears." Would, indeed, that there were a "dowsing" rod that we could use, but the choosing of a site is chiefly guess-work, yet always guess-work guided by signs and tokens, ancient worked blocks, portions of old wall, or the like. The surest indication of ancient habitation is the presence of ancient potsherds, which being both characteristic of their period and indestructible make the most descriptive of labels; intrinsically, too, they are as valueless as the stones on the hillside, so that they are not likely to have been moved except possibly downhill by the forces of denudation, and in Greece if none are to be found the spot is probably not worth consideration.

Chance often plays a part in the discovery of sites, as in the action of the river at Sparta where by erosion it brought to light treasures from the Sanctuary of Orthia, or through the cloud-burst in 1913 that laid bare the first of a series of tombs at Pachys Ammos in Crete; mostly however they

are found by diligent search, by going to and fro
in the land, and by questioning the people; the
owner of an observant eye may find what he is
seeking by tracing the origin of an ancient block
built into a modern house; for the Greek peasant
finds an old site to be the best of quarries; where
else, indeed, can he find his stone ready worked?

For the season of 1913 the British School at
Athens wished to find a prehistoric town to dig,
and a party visited Naxos in search of one. We
had a very pleasant tour round the island, but we
had no luck, finding nothing of sufficient promise
to justify an expedition. One particularly bitter
disappointment we met with there, on visiting a
site known to us as having been partially worked
a few years before. The undug portion was fairly
extensive and looked very hopeful with traces of
walls appearing and with prehistoric island pottery
lying thickly over a good area, but our hopes were
dashed by the discovery of one of those round
spaces where the Greeks of to-day use the ox,
unscripturally muzzled, to tread out their corn;
often these floors are paved, but this one was cut
down to the living rock only six inches below the
surface.

Adieu panier, vendanges sont faites. We moved
on.

Maghoula-hunting, again, was an excellent sport
in which I indulged with Mr Wace before the
excavations which resulted in his book[1]. "Mag-
houla," signifying a mound, is a modern word that
is applied to the gentle swellings on the Thessalian

[1] Wace and Thompson, *Prehistoric Thessaly.*

plain left by the *débris* of prehistoric settlements. Enquiry often gave us the direction, and we tramped the plain until we came to them, when the sherds and stone implements that we picked up gave a good indication of what lay beneath. Those sites were the easiest of any to find and the least disappointing when found that my experience has met with.

In general however the sport is weary and disheartening, and in Greece the game is becoming scarce.

CHAPTER III

QUALIFICATIONS

Meticulous care directed by common sense along the lines laid down by past experience, that is the essence of good digging; yet the ideal man to have charge of an excavation would be a very versatile person.

He should be very patient, able to hold in check any natural human desire for undue haste to seize his spoil until his sober judgment tells him that the right moment has come[1]. He should have the power of smooth organisation; and the power of delegating to others, which does not mean going away and letting the others do his work.

[1] I lay stress upon this, and by way of illustration will point to what happened at Sparta, where the presence of a site rich in votive offerings was discovered through the river's washing out samples of them from the edge of the Sanctuary of Orthia. Now the work at this spot in the first days was perhaps necessary to ascertain definitely the value of the site, but, being in its method not wholly different from the activity of the river, it produced a set of objects scientifically inarticulate, the story of which could only be told by the subsequent stratified finds; and much harm would have been done if the responsible authority had yielded to the desire to take out the plunder as fast as it could be reached, instead of having the wisdom to find out the limits of the site and then to dig it methodically, leaving the first spot till its moment came so as to save whatever stratification might there exist. It was not in the event till two years later that the place first attacked was allowed to surrender its treasures.

He should have a good power of judging the value of evidence, and enough strength of mind to give it its full weight, even when it tells against his most cherished theory; indeed he should be able to divest his mind of all theory while engaged in extracting the facts from his evidence.

He should have enough power over words to write concisely a rigidly accurate yet lucid report.

He should have a vigorous faith, and perseverance enough to carry on a while after his faith is dead.

He should have that touch of imagination that will often illuminate the true meaning of his facts, and in an archaeologist is genius.

He should be well versed in the practical side of his work, which implies skill in a good many directions, though here I have only put down the most obvious. He should have knowledge enough of rudimentary civil engineering to know how to devise the best way of removing the necessary soil, how to lay and run a light railway where its use is expedient, and how to move large weights if necessary. All these things he should be able to do, should he not have at his service a foreman who can do them: should he have such a foreman he should make very sure that the foreman's way is inferior before substituting his own, remembering that work is always better done if the method is familiar to the men doing it, that other things being equal the local way is the best way. He should be a practical surveyor in a small way, unless his expedition can afford to keep an expert at hand, for apart from the planning of his trenches and sections it may be necessary to destroy foundations that cover more important remains, and this cannot be done innocently unless a plan of them has been made that is not only accurate in itself, but can also be put accurately in its place on the plan of the whole site. For this purpose there is no need for him to be a finished draughtsman, for the final drawing can, of course, always be made by professional labour. Likewise he should be a capable draughtsman in water colours as well as in black and white. As with the planning most drawing can be done and better done professionally after the excavation is over, yet there are cases when the object is too frail to be removed intact, and the excavator's conscience is then clear only if a picture has been made before removal, for which photography is not always adequate, for all archaeological objects cannot be satisfactorily photographed, particularly if it is not possible to clean them thoroughly, because, though the camera cannot lie, it cannot make a proper distinction between dirt and design. Then he should be an efficient photographer, a photographer, not a mere taker of photographs. These last three items, planning, drawing and photography, someone must be able to do and do efficiently at a moment's notice. And though it is not, of course, necessary that the man in charge should be expert in all or any of them, these experts should be present on his staff, and if it is necessary to have special professionals always at hand, the expenses of the excavation are materially increased. It is not urged that the main planning, drawing and photography should not be done by professionals, but the main work in these branches can be done at a known time at the end of the excavation, when it is often possible to import a professional for a known amount of work, whereby the expense is much reduced. In the matter of photography moreover the archaeologist should have good experience at any rate of museum photography, that is to say, have an expert knowledge of arrangement, lighting and backgrounds, since in my experience no professional photographer can be trusted to do such work without supervision. To take but one instance; I have more than once seen photographs taken of inscriptions when an excellent negative has been quite useless because the operator did not think to arrange a side light, which would have greatly increased the legibility through the resulting shadows in the lettering. Similarly of draughtsmen. Few artists, however good, can be trusted to make archaeological drawings without supervision unless they have great experience in the kind of work required, for their eyes are not trained to the minuteness of vision, nor their minds to the inartistic accuracy that are wanted.

He should have a good knowledge of first aid to sick "anticas," which implies an elementary knowledge of chemistry. I know of an excavation where bronze axes, in order to clean off the corrosion, were put into a chemical bath which worked so efficiently as to clean away the axes.

He should know how to take those measurements of bones and skulls that are desired by anthropologists.

He should have a good book knowledge of archaeology, and at any rate, as far as possible, acquaintance with the kind of thing that he expects to find. Here a wide general familiarity is better than expert knowledge in a narrow field.

He should have the power of making swift decisions, and the readiness for responsibility that are wanted by all men at the head of serious undertakings.

He should be able readily to speak and understand the language of his workmen, and have the power of dealing with men, so as to get the best results out of them while keeping on excellent terms.

He should have tact and social charm both for dealing with his staff, for an unhappy dig is an inefficient dig, and for negotiating any difficulties that may arise.

He should have a good temper, but a stiff jaw.

Lastly, he should have digested this essay.

CHAPTER IV

THE OUTFIT AND ITS USE

The plant required by an excavation will, of course, vary with the conditions, but a list of the things that it would seem advisable to lay in may have some interest.

The main tools to be used by the men are picks, spades, knives, and baskets. In Greece a round rush basket is obtainable, being used in the mines at Laurium, which is not too large, so that when full of earth it is easily carried. It is good to have a large supply as they wear out and are useful moreover for holding small finds such as pottery, as well as for shifting the earth, and even as packing cases for the smaller finds if the journey is short, the method being to sew two together with string. The picks used should be very light and spare shafts should not be forgotten unless there is a local supply. Besides these, a crowbar or two, a sledge hammer, a few sieves and some rope are indispensable.

Indispensable also are a dumpy level, and a prismatic compass, of which the use is chiefly to take one bearing for any plan to find magnetic. I do not agree with the view that the archaeologist should trouble himself with true north unless he wants to fit his plan on to an existing map, a rare event. True north except in the case of temples and stone circles is quite immaterial, and if the work done is dated can always be obtained by any one interested.   But the stick method of ascertaining it is easy and there is no harm in employing it on a fine Sunday.   At any hour before noon a surveying pole is driven upright into the ground, and the end of the shadow is marked by a peg. A circle is drawn from the pole as centre with the then length of shadow as radius.   A watch is kept, and when in the afternoon the shadow lengthens again to touch the circle, that is to just the same length, the point at which it does so is marked by another peg.   A line is drawn from each peg to the pole, and the line that bisects the resulting angle [1] points due North and South.

For ordinary excavation work there is not much need for a theodolite and at the present time I confess that I have forgotten how to use one. Yet, since it may always be advisable in the case of a scattered site to make a survey of a longish tract of country, for which a prismatic compass is not sufficiently accurate, and since a theodolite embodies in itself a levelling instrument, it might be advisable to substitute it for the dumpy level. Over smaller areas however the system of triangles with chain or tape [2] is a more satisfactory method of making a plan for the amateur than any reading of angles, for not only is any error of any angle multiplied by the distance, but, no matter how accurately the angles are read, the angle method is fruitful of mistakes when it comes to putting the readings on paper with the help of a protractor.

[1] Euclid, Book i, Prop. 9.   [2] Appendix B.

For first aid to the finds there should be a supply of plaster of Paris and paraffin wax, and of shellac and methylated spirit for the mending of anything that, like pottery, is not damaged by a clean flame. For other objects there should be some gum or cement such as seccotine, which answers admirably where the climate is dry and warm, for the temporary mending that they need to fit them for the drawing or photography that must be done actually at the excavation, if an illustrated lecture is to be given before the full study and arrangement of results in the museum. Water however will always dissolve seccotine, so that in a damp climate its use is impossible; indeed I once knew a vase mended with it experimentally fall to pieces from the damp atmosphere after three wet days. Like shellac it has the advantage that it takes up no appreciable space, allowing a very close join, which is not the case with the porcelain cements. In Egypt I have seen limestone *Stelae* with a surface very near disintegration treated with a thin solution of tapioca with excellent results, but I have never seen stone with the same tendency to powder in a less dry climate. Still, tapioca is cheap and not bulky.

For cleaning pottery and terracotta objects a good supply of hydrochloric acid is wanted, of which the method of use is either to leave the pottery in a fairly strong solution, or to dip it in water and then to apply the acid neat with a paste brush, or to do first the one and then the other for the more obstinate points. The brushes used

in this process are not long lived. Afterwards the
acid may be neutralised by dipping the pottery
into water in which a pinch of potash has been
thrown—a very small pinch, for too much will
leave a white film difficult to remove; but where
the acid has no apparent effect on the fabric, and
otherwise it should not be used, it is probably
enough to rinse the pottery in clean water, for
within my experience no harm has ever resulted
from the omission of the potash. All unknown
wares however should be carefully tested before
applying the process, as very rarely the acid is
found to eat into the fabric; yet this is so unusual,
and in my experience so much harm is done to
delicate wares by rubbing with the brush in the
course of washing with water, that I would wish
to see acid used for all pottery found, not merely
reserved for the best, for by a patient use of it
the harmful rubbing is avoided. Moreover, if the
earth of the site is at all clinging it may be very
.hard to tell what is worthy of acid, and it is better
to shake hands with a waiter than to cut a guest.

Scrubbing brushes, large and small, and small
nail brushes are very helpful for the cleaning of
objects with a hard surface; but should the
surface be at all delicate no brush, however soft,
should be used, for the brush cannot discriminate
and, while brushing the dirt that still remains,
continues to brush the adjacent surface that it
has just cleaned, often much to its detriment.
For such cases the right tool is a needle, which
will generally be present in the excavator's personal
outfit, unless he wishes his socks to be permanently

in holes and all his buttons to be missing; nothing is better if used with a light hand and a great deal of patience, for, by rubbing gently with the side of the point and thus keeping an extremely small portion of the metal in contact with the surface, the operator can see exactly what he is doing, and need never touch again a part that is once made clean.

If it is anticipated that many small articles will be found, nests of pill boxes in large numbers are useful things to have, for an object can then be put away in its own box with its label written outside at the moment of finding; for this and other purposes cotton wool packing or better, if obtainable, wood wool should be kept.

Again if much pottery or anything that is small is expected a supply of wooden trays is very convenient, as thus a comprehensive survey of the finds is made easy; and much saving of space can be obtained, when the yield from subdivisions is small, by having a set of smaller tin trays fitting nestwise inside these. For the use of the British School at Athens, the late Director devised a portable rack for taking a number of these trays. It consisted of four stout uprights, held together by a number of cross pieces that acted as shelves, and were all numbered, and fastened by screws. These racks were used in pairs linked by battens that could also support trays.

Small bags are very useful, particularly on a pottery site, for the immediate reception of the fragments of broken but more or less complete vases, as by their use much subsequent work may

be saved, and pieces kept together that by bad
luck might go permanently astray. For other
purposes I believe trays to be better than bags,
for though it may be argued that there is more
chance of a tray's losing its label or its contents,
yet this danger with reasonable care is very slight,
and is less than that incurred by the bag when
the contents are tilted out for study. Bags should
be of canvas with a string round the neck, for
paper bags though cheaper are ephemeral and
therefore unsatisfactory.

No excavation is properly fitted out without a
good supply of squeeze paper, the unsized paper
used for taking impressions of inscriptions. This
I may use as the text of an exhortation, though it
is no part of my purpose to give hints for the
study of epigraphy, even if I were capable of
doing so, for the decipherment and interpretation
of inscriptions is a branch of archaeology by itself,
and while I do not mean to condemn the epigraphist
to be an epigraphist and nothing else, I do mean
that the versatile hero whom I have sketched will
hardly have time for the special study that alone
can give the best results in epigraphy, though he
should, of course, have a general acquaintance
with the subject. I would however exhort all
epigraphists, budding and full blown alike, to one
piece of most obvious common sense, namely, to
distrust the convenience of a copy. A copy is no
doubt necessary since neither the original inscrip-
tion nor yet, if it is a large one, a squeeze of it can
be taken conveniently into libraries for study and
the collation of parallels; but whenever possible,

even at the cost of some inconvenience, the text of inscriptions should be studied on the stones themselves, for as material for study, the stone comes first, a good squeeze second, and a copy a bad third.

Perhaps an apology is due for these remarks to a learned brotherhood whose boots I am not worthy to black. I offer it, but shall let the sentences stand.

Drawing paper, pencils, and water colours; indian ink and pens, compasses and drawing pens, these need no special mention: they can be let pass with the remark that my own experience is that there should be at least one large drawing board, and that in the matter of ink drawings to be reproduced by black and white block the most paying thing for an artist without pride is to have paper as good and as thick as possible; for much to save what appears irremediable can be done by a sharp knife, with the handle of a toothbrush kept handy to rub the scratched surface to a smoothness on which the ink will not run. It is often advisable to draw small objects larger than life size, partly for ease in working, if the detail is fine, and partly because better results in block making are got by a reduction; but they should never be published larger than actual size, for the eye is not accustomed to imagining a thing smaller than it appears and seldom manages the business properly. The draughtsman should be careful, too, if his work is to be reduced for publication, never to use too fine a line lest the block should omit it.

The photographic outfit must be adequate but need not be complex: it must however include at whatever cost of trouble, arrangements for immediate development, which failing all else can be got by making a portable dark room part of the camp baggage; no one would dream to-day of conducting a serious excavation without a competent photographer on the staff, but it is perhaps still too much the custom to trust overmuch to the success of his efforts, with the result that when he subsequently develops his plates it is to find that one or more important picture has failed. Plates, therefore, must be developed at once, and until it is known that the picture is a good one, operations must be suspended to allow of its being taken again.

At the risk of being wearisome I must repeat that the camera must not be made a fetish; that though often indispensable it is not always enough, from its fatal habit of seeing too much, so that in its pictures sometimes the essential does not stand out clearly against the unessential background: I must urge again that whenever this seems likely to happen the photograph should be supplemented by a drawing.

In spite of their extra weight, and the fear of breakage, plates should always be used in preference to films, and this not merely because of their lesser cost. The needs of an excavation are best served by a supply in three speeds, very rapid, medium, and slow, of which the first and last are essential: the first because photography on an excavation, though it must often wait for the

right position of the sun, cannot wait for the
subsidence of the wind, and in a strong wind the
only hope of successful work lies in a very rapid
plate; the last for museum work away from the
dig where the wind need not enter into the
problem, in that case a slow plate is to be preferred, because the slower the plate the easier it
is to make sure of good results, under-exposure
being practically the only danger to be guarded
against. For the same reason I like a medium
plate for use out of doors when the wind is less
violent, finding always that my more certain
results are got by using plates as slow as circumstances allow. A reliable exposure meter is a
great help. The lens or lenses used must be very
good, and the camera should have enough exten-
sion to take objects if necessary actual size. It
should also be fitted with a tilting table, as this
will not only be of great use on the excavation in
helping to get the lens into the right position for
looking into an awkward hole, but if the light is
good provides the best way of photographing
small objects, such as jewellery or potsherds; they
are put on a sheet of glass supported off the
ground by an open wooden frame with legs about
a foot high and as thin as possible to avoid
shadows; a background of white paper is placed
below and the camera is swung over so as to take
the picture directly from above; if the light is
strong enough the white background is sufficiently
brilliant to swamp any reflections off the glass,
and the fact that the background is about a foot
below the objects, brings about the disappearance

of all cast shadows which have a tendency to obscure the outlines. A good negative so taken can be used for publication as it stands, there being no occasion for the painting out of shadows that is thought to be essential but may be more damaging to the outlines than the shadows. It is very important with this ideal to get rid of the dust that is sure to fall from excavated objects when arranged for photography, and will be as good a pretext for painting the negative as actual shadows; it is often impossible to finish the job with a brush without shifting the objects which causes a renewed fall of dust, but a vulcanite fountain pen electrified by rubbing is an admirable means of picking up the last specks.

This method of photography however should not be used for anything that can be got to stand in its right position; this may entail much trouble but is worth the trouble, for only so can the really natural lighting be got. This question of natural lighting is very important, and particularly so in the case of reliefs, which should never be photographed upside down with the chief light coming from below, however much the best detail seems to demand light from that direction; much may be done by means of a simple reflector of white paper, or by flashing a mirror, but if the relief be photographed upside down almost certainly the picture seen right side up will look like an intaglio. As to backgrounds opinions differ, but my own view is in favour of white in almost every case; grey may be used if the object is so light that it is feared that the outline in the high light would not be clear against white; black should always be avoided, unless indeed the object in Euclid's phrase has breadth but no thickness, for black will take all the value from the shadows on the objects, so that in the picture they will appear quite flat, all subtleties of form being lost.

For museum photography a supply of plasticine is invaluable as it provides props of any size that can often be concealed from the camera.

From the popular point of view to increase the attractiveness of lectures there is much virtue in the colour plates of the Paget Company, though their colours do not, I think, give quite the same sense of nature as those obtained by a good Lumière autochrome, but these are of little use in the lantern being too dense and too easily damaged by heat; the scientific value of either of the methods as a record of colour is still, I think, a little uncertain and only to be relied on after careful checking with the originals.

The camera used need certainly not be larger than a half-plate, my own view is that the quarter-plate size answers all requirements, as provided that the negative is truly sharp, (no one who is not short-sighted should trust himself to work without a magnifying focusing glass), it can always be enlarged without damage to the size required for most publications. To use a larger size is, apart from the extra trouble, a needless expense. Expense however in some of the more luxurious expeditions appears to be no object, no doubt a highly laudable policy where any scientific object is to be gained, but in the matter of photography

D.

one that involves great waste to the benefit of no one but the manufacturers of photographic goods. I have not seen it with my eyes but I have heard of an excavation where a tomb is photographed not only before opening and after the contents are fully exposed, both right and proper moments for photography, but at three or four points in between; the same excavation, it is said, sees a panorama of the site taken once at least every day, that the general rate of work and gradual change in the aspect may be shown, things that can have no importance unless it is to show the supporters of the expedition that a certain amount of soil is moved every day for their money. This is photography gone mad, and the only logical outcome of it is a cinematograph operator at work all day and every day at every possibly interesting part of the site; when things reach this point the excavator will no doubt speak his notes into a dictaphone, and popular interest in archaeological work will no doubt rise high and may even reach the audience of the Picture Palace.

The outfit for an expedition intended for the utter wilds might be extended indefinitely, but a relatively civilized excavation, in a land where the services of the local artisan are available, can probably make good any omissions from this list, which is already wearisomely long.

CHAPTER V

Excavation like any other pursuit has its own special morality and it is possible to frame a new decalogue for the use of the fraternity.

1. Knowledge ascertained by proof is the only thing that really matters.

2. Do not introduce theories into your excavation work, more than is absolutely necessary. If you want to spend your time pursuing fascinating but elusive theories, well and good; but let it be your leisure time, not that devoted to your high calling.

3. Since knowledge ascertained by proof is the only thing that matters, do not let its name be taken in vain by allowing an unproved theory to take its place as a premiss in a serious argument: it is one of the subtlest temptations that beset the primrose path of theory spinning to use a conclusion that to the most sanguine eye is only probable as an ostensibly firm basis for a further edifice of speculation.

4. Work very slowly, remembering that an overtaxed staff is an inefficient staff.

5. Remember that if you once attack a site you are bound to do the best you can by its

potential store of knowledge: you must not abandon it for a caprice, because you are tired of it.

6.   Do not destroy any ancient remains.

7.   Do not mix your labels, or allow confusion among your finds; for evil so wrought has no remedy.

8.   Do not "hog"; that is, do not dig for your treasure so quickly as to risk missing half its story.

9.   Do not misrepresent your site: either by neglecting any facts however apparently trivial; or by unconsciously suppressing any facts because they are not the facts you want; or by softening down their story because it is not the story you want to hear.

10.   Do not grudge the world its right to know your facts as soon as possible; do not keep them to yourself while seeking their explanation.

Like all codes however this does not cover the whole ground, and there is more than one point in which the excavator's right course may be questioned.   How far, for instance, has he the right to destroy the remains of ancient buildings? His sixth commandment is express, yet there are times when, like homicide, destruction is expedient and right.   In any particular instance the answer must depend on the value of the building which it is proposed to destroy compared with that of the results to be obtained by demolition.

Common sense dictates that no building should be removed on a mere speculation unless certainly valueless; and a valueless building I should be

inclined to define as one that has in itself no
virtues as a specimen of the builder's art and no
peculiar features, that is not associated with any
finds, and that for this and other reasons cannot
be assigned to any certain date; except in the
case of such a building destruction should not be
indulged in, unless it is known by trials that
beneath the victim are earlier deposits that will
increase knowledge. If it is possible, as in the
case of a pavement, the building should be removed
with such care that it can be replaced afterwards.
In no case should anything be removed without
the taking of complete details for a plan and
section.

The difficulty of deciding the right course is
very great in the case of a large building that is
clearly too fine and of too much interest to admit
of even partial damage, yet is known to conceal
beneath it remains of greater value, and of value,
too, not only in themselves but for the light that
they may shed on the date and origin of the later
edifice. I am sorry that I have had no personal
experience of dealing with such a building, certainly
the most difficult problem that could confront the
excavator; but I cannot imagine any other method
of work than that of digging between the walls,
removing the floors when these consist of slabs
after first planning and numbering the slabs or
their fragments with a view to their exact replacement. The difficulty, of course, is more the greater
the size and elaboration of the building, and the
more absolute the necessity of not damaging what
is in itself a valuable monument; the treatment

however should not differ in principle from that required by the digging of a prehistoric village, where the lower operations may often be hampered by the walls of the later houses, but in such a case the paramount necessity of doing no damage to the upper structure is absent.

In the case of a large building it would, I think, be wise, orderly, and making for good work to finish first with the later building before seeking what may be below.

Another nice problem concerns the extent to which restoration of such a building may be allowed. Here I think the principle to be observed is honesty: no such restorations should be fitted as in a few years will merge indistinguishably into the old work, and strictly a small date should be cut on every new stone used. With this proviso the case for restoration, where the proposed restoration is certain, is very strong; without considering such cases as the grand staircase at Knossos, where restoration is necessary to preserve parts of the ancient structure *in situ*, there is no doubt that the uninformed imagination is helped by it; the student's expert knowledge may be help enough for him, but nine out of ten of the people who visit the monument will lack that particular aid, and for them the place is only given a meaning by the judicious replacement in some degree of the portions now missing. The only real objection to rebuilding the fallen columns of the Parthenon is the aesthetic one that we like the look of it as it is; moreover in the case of the Parthenon the argument for restoration is less strong, for enough of it is left to guide the imagination of anyone.

To the kindred question how far is it justifiable to bamboozle the museum visiting public with, say, a restored vase, I give the same answer; that a restored vase is a most desirable thing for the purpose of guiding the imagination or saving it strain only so long as the work is not carried to the point of deception; the mischief however in this particular branch is that restoration, especially of vases, is an art of which deception is the crown, which to forbid the artist to strive after is almost cruelty. I am reminded of an afternoon when I listened to the remarks of two ladies in the Ashmolean, where they have a real artist: one said, "Now I like that one. You can see there are no joins, it must all be real." The ladies were short, but I could just see over the lip of the Cretan vase in question, and on the inner surface the network of joins and the pieces replaced by plaster were clear to me; I said nothing, but meditated on morality.

In the case of drawings for publication I am inclined to draw the bounds of what is permissible rather wider from the confines of strict truth than in dealing with the actual object; the two limits that I would then impose are that the skill of the restoration should be so restricted that no doubt should arise as to which portions are or are not genuine, and that there should be good ground and warrant for the restored part; in the case of the actual object I would admit no fanciful restoration. It is this last restriction that I think it

justifiable to remit in the case of drawings; their
object is to rouse interest and they best fulfil it
when they show not only the present condition of
the object, but what it was like, or failing that
what it was probably like, in the past. A sacrifice
to truth may be made by the simultaneous publication of a photograph. The reason for the
distinction is obvious; in the case of a drawing
we are not poisoning the fountain-head of truth,
but the object remains untouched to be studied
by those sufficiently interested. If it is true that
such study has sometimes led to profound astonishment, this astonishment so far from condemning
the illustration that caused it is its real justifica-
tion. Take the case of a fragment of a Kamares
vase. The fragment is too small for the shape of
the vase to be plain except to a student of Middle
Minoan pottery; the design is in white, crimson,
and orange-red on a black ground, but time has
so wrought on it that none of the colours not even
the dark ground have their true value except, if
we are lucky, at one point for each; the white is
all gone but for one speck, but has preserved the
surface of the underlying black so that the design
can be seen by shifting the fragment to reflect the
light. What value in such a case would be
possessed by an absolutely accurate drawing? It
would convey no meaning, even if it could be
made, for how can a drawing without exaggeration
show traces that can indeed be certainly seen, but
only by the sharpest trained eyesight? In such
a case the drawing should aim at showing the
probable appearance of the complete vase when in

use; the full form will be shown, those parts that are restored being coloured fainter than the rest, where the original tone should be given to the colours; in any place on the existing portions where the design is not clear, there is no excuse for not indicating the doubt, but it is, I think, legitimate on the restored part in the case of uncertainty to supply what is most probable. In his astonishment, when confronted with the original, the man who has only known the drawing may think that he has had his leg pulled. It is not so, for while an absolutely true drawing would have told him nothing, the restoration has made him free of the knowledge gleaned from wide study. His astonishment is the measure of the value of the drawing.

CHAPTER VI

The excavation is over, all possible subdivisions and all necessary notes, drawings and photographs have been made; over, too, is the period of study in the museum, and what now lies before the excavator is the publication of the results. Somewhere the complete record of the work done should be kept for reference in case subsequent work should reveal interests in the material unsuspected at the time, but it is not advisable to lay all the details open in a publication. For my labour has been vain if I have not made it clear that to do his work properly the excavator must note down all possible observations whether their interest is apparent at the time or not; many of these, probably the greater number, will in the end prove valueless, and it would be like giving a thirsty man salt water to drink to serve them up to a public hungry for knowledge. There is too great a tendency in modern archaeological work to swamp the interest of the results with a flood of detailed evidence, that makes the dreariest reading, and often is its own undoing, for only those conclusions that reach the highest point of interest can survive. To take an instance: an excavation of quite moderate extent might easily embrace a hundred and fifty sections more or less productive, each of which might have six or seven vertical sections; at headquarters there should be a record of the contents of these thousand subdivisions, but to print page after page of these details would be nauseating. Few would be found to read such a record, and on them the result would be to kill the interest that it is desired to provoke. To print a few typical examples to show the manner in which evidence is presented would be excellent, but to display the whole is little short of indecent. It may be objected that such a thing has never yet been done, but none the less, it is the regrettable modern tendency to describe at ever greater and more unnecessary length the individual bricks before proceeding to raise the edifice of knowledge gained; the tendency is regrettable partly because it makes for the belief that one of the most fascinating pursuits belongs to the category of dry and mouldy occupations, partly because it raises the standard of the cost of archaeological publications. If it is objected that without a presentation of all his evidence a man cannot expect to command belief, the answer is, that if he is to be presumed to be a liar he may be suspected to have manufactured his evidence. He must, it is true, give a *résumé* of the evidence to show that he is not making mistakes in his conclusions; it is not, for instance, enough for him to say that he is sure pottery A is later than pottery B, he must also tell why he thinks so, namely that over a wide area he has found A above B, but there is no need and very good

reason against his producing pages of printed
matter showing *A* above *B*. The whole thing
comes down to the advisability of concision in the
interests first of the reader and through him of
the science of archaeology. A possible exception
comes in the case of a cemetery, for the contents
of a tomb are one fact not to be separated either
in a museum or in a publication; but as nothing
is more dreary than a long catalogue of the
contents of mediocre tombs, the excavator should
exercise a strict censorship over these facts and
be very sure that each is of interest before he lets
it see the light.

I believe that the right method of publication
is to give an example or two of the naked evidence
(and this in the case of a stratified site can perhaps
be best done diagrammatically by means of a
section across the plan) [1], then a clear account of
the facts shown by the evidence, and lastly a state-
ment of the conclusions founded on the facts, the
whole in the fewest possible words compatible with
good English. Then the excavator's duty is done.

Should he elect to supplement his facts by an
essay, or essays, embodying the parallels that he
can collect, or the theories that he spins about
them, the excellence or otherwise of his attempts
will depend upon his parts; but in any case this
is an added act of his as a student of archaeology,
no part of his duty as an excavator; that duty is
to publish his facts as quickly as is consistent with
thorough study that all the world may be at
liberty to spin theories, for the sooner new facts

[1] See Appendix C.

are presented for general study, the better served is the cause of History. In the past, facts have often been held up too long that their discoverer might himself publish with them their explanation.

So much, then, about the final publication, but what should be the policy for preliminary reports? There are, I think, no good grounds for any deviation from the policy of promptitude and brevity, except that in view of the need of stimulating public interest a certain amount of theory and interpretation may be allowed with an unfolding of the hopes aroused by the work done to date. But some men will publish preliminary reports, yet will not put into them all that they might. That is promptitude sacrificed to brevity, and it is that same need of keeping the public's interest that is the cause; for with the necessity for a full and final publication before their eyes they have been tempted to refrain from making known at once their most interesting results from a fear lest the final work should lose interest by seeming mere repetition. It is a question of pure expediency as to when the best effect can be produced. Yet even from that point of view the temptation should, I think, be resisted, if only on the principle of "gather ye rosebuds while ye may," and all finds be allowed to come out as quickly as possible; for time in any case may wither their interest, while there is always the glorious chance that to-morrow may have treasures in store so radiant as to quite outshine to-day's. Should that happen there is a pure loss of effect, and, though in the subsequent triumph it may not be missed, this year's subscriptions may have suffered. Thus even on the low ground of expediency the case is weak against making preliminary reports as full of matter as time and the conditions allow. And on any other ground there is no case at all; for the fear of making mistakes should not be a deterrent: care should of course as always be taken not to permit surmise to wear the garb of fact, but the excavator need not pretend to omniscience, and the due correction of mistakes later on in the light of fuller evidence does not discredit our mystery.

CHAPTER VII

EPILOGUE

By way of epilogue I may perhaps venture a short word on the question much discussed in certain quarters, whether in the work of excavation it is a good thing to have co-operation between men and women. I have no intention of discussing whether or no women possess the qualities best suited for such work; opinions, I believe, vary on the point, but I have never seen a trained lady excavator at work, so that my view if expressed would be valueless. Of a mixed dig however I have seen something, and it is an experiment that I would be reluctant to try again; I would grant if need be that women are admirably fitted for the work, yet I would uphold that they should undertake it by themselves.

My reasons are two-fold and chiefly personal. In the first place there are the proprieties; I have never had a very reverent care for these abstractions, but I think it is not everywhere sufficiently realised that the proprieties that have to be considered are not only those that rule in England or America, but those of the lands where it is proposed to dig; the view to be considered is the view of the inhabitants, Greek, Turk, or Egyptian. My chief reasons, I said, were personal, but I hasten to add that they have nothing to do with the particular ladies with whom I was associated; should these lines meet their eyes I hope they will believe me when I say that before and after the excavation I thought them charming; during it however because they, or we, were in the wrong place their charm was not seen. My objection lies in this, that the work of an excavation on the dig and off it lays on those who share in it a bond of closer daily intercourse than is conceivable, except perhaps in the Navy where privacy is said to be unobtainable, except for a captain; with the right men that is one of the charms of the life, but between men and women, except in chance cases, I do not believe that such close and unavoidable companionship can ever be other than a source of irritation; at any rate I believe that, however it may affect women, the ordinary male at least cannot stand it. It is true that it might also be a source of matrimony, but as that would mean a temporary end to the serious work of two members of the expedition, it can hardly be used as an argument for co-operation. Marriage apart, and I can imagine a man conducting a small excavation very happily with his wife, mixed digging I think means loss of easiness in the atmosphere and consequent loss of efficiency. A minor, and yet to my mind weighty, objection lies in one particular form of constraint entailed by the presence of ladies, it must add to all the strains of an excavation, and they are many, the further strain of politeness and self-restraint in moments of stress, moments that will occur on the best regulated dig, when you want to say just what you think without translation, which before ladies, whatever their feelings about it, cannot be done.

APPENDIX A

THE USE OF THE DUMPY LEVEL

The Dumpy Level is a revolving telescope with an attached spirit level set up on a tripod and made perfectly horizontal by means of screws. A board marked in metres is held vertically on the spot of which the height is to be ascertained, and the reading is taken through the telescope, the figure read being that cut by the hair stretched horizontally across the eyepiece, which for some reason unknown to me has no reverser so that the figures are read upside down, a trick however to which the eye soon becomes accustomed. The figure thus obtained is the difference in height between the chosen spot and the telescope in that position. Clearly before the reading can have any value the height of the telescope must be found by taking a reading with the board placed on a known fixed mark within range of the operations, to which mark it is best to give an arbitrary height of say 100 m. Then a simple sum in subtraction is all that is necessary: say the reading on the mark A, as in Fig. 4, is 3 m. and the readings on the chosen spots C and D are 4 m. and 4·25 m. respectively, C and D are 1 m. and 1·25 m. respectively below A, and have therefore the arbitrary heights of 99 m. and 98·75 m. This subtraction of the lower from the higher reading will always give the difference in height between the mark and the chosen spot; but should the reading on the mark show the higher figure the mark is in that case of course lower than the chosen spot, and the difference must then be added to, not taken from, the known height of the mark to find the height of the chosen spot. It should be remembered that all that any one reading gives is the vertical distance between the bottom of the board and the level of the telescope. Should the actual height of the mark above sea level be known this may, of course, be used, but whether this is so or not is immaterial, for the purpose of fixing relative heights on the site is equally well served by an arbitrary figure.

When the operations move so far as to make it possible to read the board only when placed on one of the two necessary positions either on the mark or on the spot in question but not on both, that is to say when the

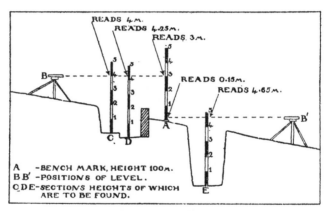

Fig. 4. The use of the Dumpy Level.

vertical difference between the two has become more than the length of the board (and the workable length of the board can hardly exceed 5 metres) a new mark must be chosen. A hilly site indeed may need several. The vertical distance between the second mark and the first must be found, and this is done (Fig. 5) by setting up the telescope so that a reading can just be taken on the lowest figures at the bottom of the board (reading 1, e.g. 0·25 m.), and then moving the board down-hill till its top can just be read with the telescope in the same position (reading 2, e.g. 4·80 m.). The subtraction of 1 from 2 gives the vertical distance that the board has been moved downwards (4·55 m.). If such a position satisfies the requirements for the new mark the work is done. If not the telescope must be moved down till again the bottom figures of the board still held in the new position come within its scope (reading 3, e.g. 0·60 m.). The board is then moved down again and a fourth reading taken (reading 4, e.g. 4·85 m.), when the subtraction of 3 from 4 will give the distance covered by this second

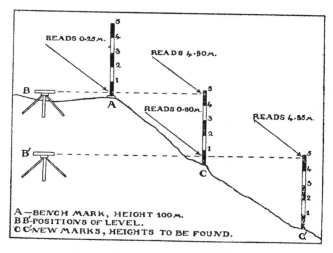

Fig. 5. The use of the Dumpy Level.

move (4·25 m.). And so on. The work must always end with the board on the new mark, and an addition of the various distances that the board has been moved gives the difference in height between the two marks (4·55 m. + 4·25 m. = 8·80 m., making the height of the second mark in the example 91·20 m.). To find a new mark at a higher level the process is the same but reversed.

For the sake of accuracy it is a good thing to work out the difference between two marks again in the opposite direction.

All marks should be inscribed with their heights when possible. Of course whenever the telescope is set up readings can be taken on any number of desired spots, but the reading on the mark must never be forgotten as it is this alone that will correlate the readings of to-day with those taken yesterday when the telescope was set up at a different level.

APPENDIX B

The diagram shown in Fig. 6 is intended to make clear the measurements necessary for planning a rect-angular enclosure within which is a round tower, by the method of triangles.

It is clear that the details may vary, and that if there are left only foundations over which the measuring tape can be carried many measurements can be taken that would be impossible if the walls were standing.

The measurements necessary are:

(*a*)   If there are only foundations.

   (1)   For the enclosure:

$D—C$, $A—D$, $A—C$ to fix the position of A; $B—C$, $B—D$ to fix B; $D—E$, $C—E$ to fix E; $F—C$, $F—D$ to fix F; $E—H$, $F—H$ to fix H; $E—G$, $F—G$ to fix G; $F—X$, $F—Y$, $B—V$, $B—Z$ to fix the positions of the corners of the doorway $XYVZ$ on the lines FG, BC. (As a check the thickness of the walls can be measured at various points.)

   (2)   For the tower:

$H—Q$, $H—R$, $E—O$, $E—P$ to fix $QROP$, extra points that should be taken because the triangles ELF, HIG are too flat for accuracy; $E—K$, $H—K$ to fix K; $O—L$,

P—L to fix L; F—M, G—M to fix M; Q—I, R—I to
fix I; Q—N, R—N to fix N (four points are the
minimum required to pin down a circle); Q—S, R—S
to fix S; O—T, P—T to fix T; S—W, T—W to fix W;
S—U, T—U to fix U.

(The method works thus: to fix the position of A a
start is made by laying down the line D—C, then two
circles are drawn, one with centre D and radius D—A,

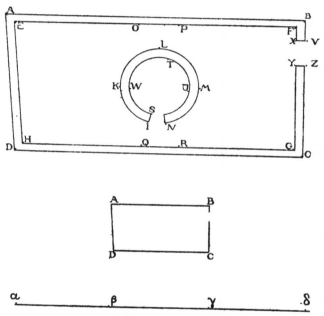

Fig. 6. Specimen Plan showing measurements needed.

the other with centre C and radius C—A, the whole
being drawn to scale; the point where the circles cut
one another is A. To find the centre and describe the
complete circle after fixing the points $KLMN$—the fourth
point is necessary but only as a check—reference should
be made to Euclid, Book III, Prop. 25.)

(*b*)   If the walls are standing.

(1)   For the outside of the enclosure:

(An artificial base line a—δ must be laid down and two points β, γ taken on it such that a straight line can be drawn from A to β and from B to γ.)

a—β, a—γ, a—δ to fix $a\beta\gamma\delta$; a—A, β—A to fix A; a—D, β—D to fix D; γ—B, δ—B to fix B; γ—C, δ—C to fix C; B—V, B—Z to fix V and Z, the outside corners of the doorway.

(2)   For the inside of the enclosure:

H—Q (putting Q so that it is in a line with I—S), H—R, H—G to fix Q and R; E—H, E—Q to fix E; F—R, F—G to fix F; F—X, F—Y to fix X and Y, the inside corners of the doorway.

(To fit the inside to the outside measure the thickness of the walls.)

(3)   For the tower:

F—O, F—P to fix O and P; O—L, P—L to fix L; E—K, H—K to fix K; F—M, G—M to fix M; Q—I, R—I to fix I; Q—N, R—N to fix N; Q—S—T to fix T (if Q has been taken in a line with I and S the position of T can be fixed at the point where that line continued meets the wall); T—W, S—W to fix W; T—U, S—U to fix U.

APPENDIX C

GRAPHIC PUBLICATION

This plan and section, imaginary, but founded on fact, give a sketch of the evidence in the domain of pottery, which from its indestructible nature in general provides the best evidence, that is warrant for the following facts. To the known period that is covered by the pottery a belongs the house that is built on the rock; at this spot there was no earlier building. Subsequently, at the period covered by the known pottery β the site was still inhabited, and traces of what was perhaps a clay floor suggest that there was a house built on the ruins of the first, but if so its walls have disappeared. The pottery γ gives the period at which the upper comparatively well preserved house flourished. The local style of ware, known as such by its overwhelming quantity both in painted and domestic pieces of identical clay, can be

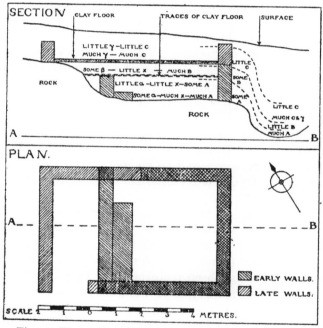

Fig. 7. Plan and section to illustrate graphic publication.

traced in its development through the three periods A, B, C. It is a piece of pure luck that the imported presence of the known wares a, β, γ links this local ware with the outside world and perhaps supplies it with some absolute dates, but their known development only corroborates but is not needed to establish the development of the series A, B, C and its relation to the houses, both of which are settled by its own positions in the strata. Incidentally the strange ware x is noted; this is not local but is not otherwise known; it is clear that it was imported in great quantities during the A period, when study shows that it was also imitated in the local clay, and that the supply diminished during the B period, and was entirely cut off before the C period was reached. These facts are of no kind of interest at present but may prove of inestimable value if at a future date large quantities of the x ware turn up in surroundings that have otherwise nothing to date them.

This section is also designed to illustrate a very possible state of affairs where the value of minute subdivision is apparent. Outside the east wall there is a steep depression in the rock of which the modern surface showed no indication. This has caused the strata of deposits to dip in geological fashion, and though perhaps this might not happen as regularly as I have shown it for the sake of clearness, there might well be enough dip to produce the appearance of complete confusion if the whole distance from the wall to the point B were dug in one piece; for, after C pottery had been decently followed by B and A, more C mixed with γ would most improperly appear followed closely by more B, all coming at a lower level than the A first found; the inference from this would be that the place had been disturbed, the only comfortable fact being the quantity of A ware at the bottom of all. It is true that a guess at the true state of things might be made when the existence of the pocket in the rock became clear, and a lucky note that the first A was found close to the wall where the rock subsequently proved to come higher might confirm the guess; my point is that the necessity for guessing should be avoided so far as possible, and that by digging the space in two divisions the confusion would to a great extent be obviated, and there would be hope of obtaining two fairly reasonable sets of strata though at different levels, which difference of level the pocket in the rock would afterwards explain. If the existence of the pocket could be known beforehand the subdivision would of course be made; unfortunately the contour of the virgin soil is the last thing to become clear, and what I wish to emphasize is that the only way to reduce to a minimum the confusion due to its vagaries is to assume their existence beforehand and subdivide.

APPENDIX D

ON THE CAUSES OF DISHONESTY AMONG WORKMEN

One great difference between Greece and Egypt in the conditions of excavation is the prevailing dishonesty among the Egyptian workmen. Stealing in Greece and Italy is an evil rarely met with, in Egypt it is a matter of course against which the excavator must guard himself as best he can. He is between the devil and the deep sea; he may choose to insure that he gets what he finds by paying the workmen the full market value of the object; that is a snare of the devil, for so he runs a good risk of getting also what he has not found, as, from what I have seen of the conditions of digging in Egypt, particularly of tomb digging, I think it would be very hard to detect the salting of the site with objects genuine enough but coming from other excavations where "backshish" is not given. To my mind the risk of such salting is not to be borne, cutting as it does at the root of all scientific work; yet if the more scientific course is taken and the excavator trusts only to ceaseless surveillance, though he is certain about what he does get, he knows that the deep sea of Oriental subtlety will swallow half of his legitimate spoil.

The causes of this fundamental difference are not obscure. They are to be found not so much in the difference between European and Oriental ideas on the right methods of acquiring property, though the laxer notions of the East may be a contributory cause, as in the European's freedom from temptation. In classical lands the finding of objects with a great market value, particularly the finding of gold, is very rare. Yet the real freedom from temptation is provided by the strict administration of the laws against the exportation of antiquities[1]. The Greek law of antiquities for instance is not ideal; it is said to cause the destruction of many chance finds from the finder's reluctance to undergo the quite unprofitable trouble involved in declaration; but it has completely muzzled the dealer, for the export of valuable antiquities can only be done in the strictest secrecy at very great risk. The result is that in practice there is no market for a stolen "antica"; it is a dangerous possession, and the means for getting rid of it are not ready to hand. In Egypt I believe the matter is different. When the authorities have taken what they will of the finds the excavator can do what he likes with the rest; there is no embargo on the export of antiquities; the dealer is supreme, and the consequent ready market for stolen goods makes the temptation irresistible.

Freedom of export has been the source, too, of another evil to Egyptian archaeology. With the power of getting what he found for himself or his employers the excavator's

[1] Nevertheless the Greek authorities might be more generous to excavators in the matter of granting them duplicates. The notion at the bottom of their policy, and it is a true notion, of course is that the antiquities like the scenery are the country's wealth, and a bait to attract strangers. But Crete, for instance, would gain far more by the advertisement of having representative collections of Minoan pottery in the museums of Europe than she will by trying to insure that the Candia Museum remains unique in every respect; it has enough unique objects to insure its importance for ever.

attention was in the past too often focused exclusively on the objects, with neglect of the conditions of their finding.   Where there is no power of export and consequently no personal advantage to hope for but knowledge, though he may have found it harder to get funds for his work, the excavator's attention has naturally been devoted more to the development of scientific digging.

APPENDIX E

ARCHAEOLOGICAL INFERENCES

I have not burdened this work with a number of instances of the kind of reasoning demanded of the excavator for the interpretation of his facts, because these will generally find a place in the published results and my object has rather been to explain what may not

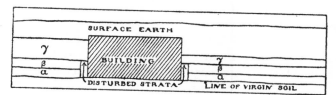

Fig. 8.   Section to show how the date of a building relative to the surrounding deposits can be inferred from their positions.

find a place there, namely the methods to be used just for arriving at the facts; but I have drawn Fig. 8 to illustrate one piece of reasoning as a sample, choosing it because of its clearness and because it would always hold true.   The facts are that there is a building having its foundations resting on virgin soil and surrounded by well stratified deposits.   The two strata at the bottom α and β are of equal height on each side of the building but the uppermost deposit γ is found to be much thicker on one side than on the other. Moreover in the very near neighbourhood of the building the two lower deposits are found to be disturbed but not so the uppermost layer. The certain inference apart from any other evidence is that the building was erected after the deposits α and β had been laid down but before the deposit γ; for nothing but the presence of the building can account for the much greater thickness of γ found on the one side of it, and since nothing of the kind is observable in α and β it is reasonable to suppose that the cause was absent at the time that they came into being, while their disturbed state is an added proof that trenches for the foundations were dug down through them. I would not say that an even level of deposits is always sufficient ground for assuming that the foundations that go through them are necessarily later in date, for it is only probable that the levels would be affected in some way by the building if it were present; it is certain however that whenever a difference in depth is observed between the undisturbed strata on the two sides of a building the building was there to cause it.

This point will have been recognised as having been made in connection with the archaic altar and the later temple at the Sanctuary of Orthia at Sparta[1].

I remember another piece of reasoning on which hung an important question of chronology in connection with the excavation at Zerelia, the first of the prehistoric Thessalian sites dug by Mr Wace. Mixed with the uppermost layer of prehistoric deposit and about half a metre, if my memory serves me, beneath the surface were found a few late Mycenaean sherds. Scattered on the surface these would of course have told no more than that at some subsequent time they had found their way there; it was held however that, mixed as they were with the prehistoric deposit and lying well below the

---

[1] Dawkins, *B. S. A.* xvi, pp. 27 and 32.

surface, which being that of a mound was likely to have suffered from denudation in the course of ages rather than to have been built up, they were contemporary with the accompanying deposits and good evidence for the final date of the prehistoric period there. But I have since wondered whether, being so few, they were strong enough to bear that burden, on the principle that any one thing may have got anywhere.

INDEX

Acid (hydrochloric), use of, 41, 42
Aim, excavator's general, 1
Antiquities, dealers in, 74; Egyptian and Greek law of, 74
Ashmolean museum, 55
Athens, British school at, 32, 43

Backshish, 73
Bags, 43
Baskets, 24, 39
Breakages, 16, 27
Brushes, use and dangers of, 42
Building (valueless), definition of, 53
Buildings, destruction of, 52 ff.; restoration of, 54

Candia, museum of, 74 (note)
Cements, 41
Cemetery, method of finding, 23; publication of, 60
Chemistry, 37
Cleaning of objects, 26, 37, 41, 42
Collectors, 8, 27, 74
Compass, prismatic, 39, 40
Consistency of finds, ix
Cretan pottery, 2, 56, 74
Crete, 31, 74
Crimes (archaeological), 1, 2, 5, 13, 14, 19, 21, 22, 23, 24, 29, 36, 42, 51 ff.
"Cyrenaic" vases, 9

Day-book, 30
Dealers in antiquities, 74
Decalogue, the digger's, 51
Destruction of ancient remains, 36, 52, 53
Diagrams, use of, 17, 27
Digging, essence of good, 34; right method of, 11; theory of, 7
Draughtsmen, need of supervision, 37
Drawing, 36; for reproduction, 45

Drawing-board, 45
Drawing-paper, 45
Drawings, restoration in, 55 ff.
Dugas, Mons., 9, 11
Dump, site for, 23
Dumping, means for, 23; objections to rapid, 24; objections to elaborate system, 25
Dumpy level, 11, 39, 40, 65 ff.

Egypt, vii, 15, 73, 74
Epigraphists, 43
Evenness in digging, importance of, 13
Evidence, kinds of contrasted, 8
Excavations, mixed, 63, 64
Excavator, his aim, 1; his duty in publication, 60; his ideal, 7; his morality, 51; his philosophy, 26; his point of view, danger to, 25; his qualifications, 34 ff.
Expenses, possibility of reducing, 36, 37
Experience, need of, viii

Finds, first aid to, 25, 37; importance of establishing positions of, 2, 6; method of establishing positions of, 11; neglect of, 1; packing in baskets, 39; potential importance of all, 3
Floors, 11
Foreman, 35
Fragile objects, help for, 25
Frescoes, 30

Germans, 22
Greece, 8, 10, 16, 19, 73
Greeks, modern, 32

Haste, harm of, 4
Hillside, dangers of, 24
"Hogging," 5, 52
Hours of work, 19

Skulls, measurement of, 38
Soil, importance of changes in, 17; virgin, importance of reaching, 21; virgin, importance of contours of, 7, 72
Sparta, 10, 18, 31, 34, 76
Squeeze paper, 44
Staff, need of adequate, in museum, 5; need of adequate, on the excavation, 4
Strata, effect of buildings on, ix, 76; not always provided, ix
Stratification, evidence from, 8; importance of, ix; use of paint to distinguish, 29
Style, evidence from, 8
Subdivision, necessity for, 11
Supervision, of excavation, 19; of draughtsmen and photographers, 37
Surveying, 35, 68
Sympathies, need of wide, 1

Tapioca, use as preservative of stone, 41
Theodolite, 40
Theories, when harmful, 35
Theory of digging, 7; wrong, 4
Thessaly, 33, 76

Threshing floors, 32
Tips, system of, 16
Tombs, publication of, 60; search for, 23
Tools, 15, 16, 39
Toothbrush handle, use in drawing, 45
Top, necessity of working from, 14
"Toutou" vases, 28
Toutoús, Geórgios, 28
Trays, 43
Trenches, advantages over pits, 21
Trials, 20; wrong method, 22

Vases, "Cyrenaic," 9; Laconian V, 28; Minoan, 2, 56, 74; "Minyan," 3
Vulcanite, 48

Wace, A. J. B., Esq., 32, 76
Walls, old under modern, 21
Wood, use of for labels, 28
Wool, cotton, 43; wood, 43
Workmen, carelessness of, 16, 19; dishonesty of, 73; laziness of, 14

Zerelia, evidence for chronology of, 76